GW00640660

THE TIME OF THE END

THE TIME OF THE END

MILLENARIAN BELIEFS IN ULSTER

MYRTLE HILL

THE BELFAST SOCIETY
IN ASSOCIATION WITH
THE ULSTER HISTORICAL FOUNDATION

ACKNOWLEDGEMENTS

I WOULD LIKE TO THANK all those who engaged with me in discussions of millenarianism over the past year, but particularly James Donnelly, John Gray, Gareth Higgins, John Lynch and Gail Walker. Thanks to Reg for being there.

The staff of the Linen Hall Library were, as always, of great help in locating materials, and thanks are also due to the following for permission to reproduce illustrations: the Chester Beatty Library, Dublin; the Linen Hall Library, Belfast; the Office of Public Works and the National Gallery, Dublin; the *Illustrated London News*; the Imperial War Museum, London; the *Belfast Telegraph*.

First published 2001
by the Belfast Society, c/o Linen Hall Library,
17 Donegall Square North, Belfast BT1 5GD
in association with the Ulster Historical Foundation
12 College Square East, Belfast, BT1 6DD

Distributed by
the Ulster Historical Foundation

ISBN 0-9539604-2-0

Printed by the Northern Whig
Design by Dunbar Design

CONTENTS

The Four Horsemen of the Apocalypse
Woodcut by Albrecht Dürer
Courtesy of the Chester Beatty Library, Dublin

INTRODUCTION

Hasten, Lord; cut short the work in righteousness.
Take Thy great power and reign[1]

APOCALYPTIC PROPHECY is nothing new. As Damian Thompson points out in his wonderfully readable *The End of Time*, 'the theme of epochs brought to an end by human wickedness, and the closeness to the end, emerges as the common denominator of the world's historic religions.'[2] Throughout time and across continents, men – and women – have searched for signs of the 'end of history' in sacred texts, natural phenomena and social and political convolutions. While such beliefs are not part of the intellectual mainstream in our own age, this does not mean they are absent from it. Indeed, the approach of the third millennium witnessed an upsurge of fearful expectancy, centred particularly on the year 2000. Publishing houses, television and the media responded enthusiastically, feeding the popular imagination with books, programmes and articles devoted to the interpretation of theological, mystical, astrological and other prophecies which converged to highlight the significance of this nicely-rounded number. And although New Year's Day 2000 dawned without evidence of divine disruption, speculations on the ways that the world will end continue; these include environmental catastrophe, planetary collision or computer-generated shutdown. A proliferation of cults and sects in almost every continent predicts, with ever-growing frequency, divine and cataclysmic intervention in the affairs of mankind. While mainstream society prefers to view such groups as fanatics or extremists, dangerous but deluded, the belief that the world will end with a terrifying cosmic battle between good and evil lies at the heart of the faith of millions.

The belief that Christ will personally return to earth to reign for one thousand years alongside the saints has, after all, been the basis of Christian hope since the crucifixion, and resonates through the two-thousand year history of the Christian faith. In the midst of persecution, the first disciples and the apostolic church interpreted the teaching of Jesus literally, and eagerly awaited his Second Coming, this time to rule in glory and majesty. When this did not immediately happen, Christians turned to what they regarded as sacred and inspired literature – the books of Daniel and Revelation, the Apocrypha (books not held equal to the Sacred Scriptures) and the 'synoptic Apocalypse' (the words of Jesus himself) – to search for clues to the timing of the creation of a new world.[3]

Revelation has been particularly central to millennial belief. Also known as the Book of the Apocalypse, this surrealistic account of the vision of John is believed to set out the entire history of the church in symbolic form, concluding with a terrifyingly spectacular description of the cosmic battle between Good and Evil, Christ's glorious return and his one thousand year reign on earth, followed by a general resurrection and the final judgement before God. The stakes are high – everlasting life or eternal damnation in a lake of fire – and the images both vivid and mysterious enough to have preoccupied scholars and enthusiasts alike for two thousand years. The meaning of the seven seals, the breaking of which sets in train a series of disasters; the identity of the 'beast whose number is 666' – known as the Antichrist – have been seen as relevant to every age since John's recording of his vision. Those who have been identified as the Antichrist include Nero, Napoleon, Hitler, Gorbachev and even Margaret Thatcher, though the Papacy has long held pride of place. Despite the fearful nature of the predictions, however, it is important to remember that the Book of Revelation finishes with John's entreaty, 'Even so, come Lord Jesus'[4] – a plea echoed by Christians down the centuries. For the 'New World' which Christ's coming will usher in is to be characterised by peace, harmony and joyous reward for earthly suffering.

Even within the Christian tradition, however, there is considerable diversity of opinion around these texts and their interpretation. There are those, for example, who believe that the words of Revelation relate to the specific context of the first century in which they were written and are not transferable to the third millennium.[5]

Others have insisted that the biblical prophecies are shrouded in mystery into which human minds should not dabble, and warn of the 'dangers of speculation'. Amongst millenialists themselves, there is disagreement over whether Christ's return will precede the establishment of his kingdom on earth, or come after the millennium has been established through the work and teachings of the church. Either way, the interpretation of the ancient prophecies as directly relevant to contemporary life carries important implications for one's view of the world. For example, the latter position (postmillenialist) implies the ultimate success of gospel preaching and the gradual victory of good over evil. Premillenialists, on the other hand, would expect things on earth to be going from bad to worse, with the Antichrist increasing his hold on society before Christ dramatically returns to defeat evil at the Battle of Armageddon. Christians thus need to be prepared for His return at any moment, and the text – 'Be ye, therefore, ready also, for the Son of Man cometh, at an hour when ye think not' – has been the subject of countless sermons, a centrepiece of revivalism, a message proclaimed on hoardings to promise the faithful and warn the careless.

Nonetheless, while numerous cults and sects – from seventeenth-century Fifth Monarchists to the twentieth-century followers of David Koresh in Waco – have anticipated the Second Coming with passionate and dramatic ardour; within mainstream Christianity the final fulfilment of prophecy is an integral, but mainly subdued, aspect of faith. Local circumstances can, however, be an important factor. Seventeenth-century Protestant settlers in Ireland, for example, surrounded on all sides by hostile papists, referred to themselves in biblical terms as Israelites entering a land covenanted by God.[6] This identification with God's 'chosen people', the 'elect', ousted from their homeland, but destined to be 'vindicated, exalted and restored to a transformed Israel',[7] resonates particularly through the history of Irish Presbyterianism, with the return of the Jews to Israel seen by many to be the penultimate event of history. Both the Presbyterian Westminster Confession of Faith, drawn up in 1649, and the 1615 Articles of the Church of Ireland refer to the Pope as the Antichrist, and theological, as well as popular anti-Catholicism has been a constant feature of the Ulster Protestant mentality, thus setting Irish Protestants apart from their mainstream British counterparts.

Although the attempt to align God's calendar with that of man requires some convoluted reasoning, the numerical clues believed to be contained within the scriptures have given rise to a vast range of predictions of the timing of the world's end. With every numerical figure believed to possess a hidden significance, the possibilities are endless.[8] One of the earliest to interpret earthly events as the unravelling of the prophecies, and to suffer grievous disappointment, was Montanus, writing in AD156, and the centuries are dotted with recurrent episodes of expectant excitement followed by disillusionment and the reworking of complex calculations. William Miller was convinced that the world would end between 21 March 1843 and 21 March 1844; when it did not one of his followers provided a new date – 22 October 1844. Such specificity was both inspirational and disastrous; those waiting to ascend from the mountaintop clothed in white robes never recovered from the 'Great Disappointment', nor the ridicule to which they were subjected. The precise dating of the end of time still occurs: an elderly Nassau engineer, for example, named 3 October 1998 as the final day.[9] Prophetic utterances are more usually, however, confined to general warnings relating to contemporary natural and international catastrophes. The words of County Tyrone minister, the Rev. W.J. Christie in 1866, were more typical:

> There have been signs in the heavens above and in the earth beneath, all of which utter the warning cry so clearly and unmistakably that if any are found locked in the slumber of careless indifference they will be left wholly without excuse.[10]

Social and political disruption and a feeling of vulnerability seem to characterise those periods when intellectual theological interpretation and popular fears merge in a reading of contemporary events as part of a more universal confrontation between good and evil. Thus war or revolution have frequently been interpreted as signs of the imminence of the last days – civil war in seventeenth-century England, the French Revolution, the rise of Communism, even the onset of the European Union – have all led to apocalyptic speculation of varying degrees.

As Marina Benjamin says, the concepts and images of millennial ideology are available to all levels of society:

> The scholarly exegete, the self-proclaimed Messiah, the evangelical

> preacher, the prophet of hope, the prophet of doom, the Mormon missionary, and the restorer of Israel all employed the same body of religious ideas, spoke the same religious language, pondered the same set of biblical images.[11]

However, the more one studies the phenomenon, the more difficult it seems to ascertain why millenarian movements arise in some periods, or places, and not in others. While in almost every age there are individuals who turn to the prophecies to make sense of current events, there does not seem to be a discernible pattern which fits all cases of more widespread millennial fervour. The aim of this publication is to trace the history of millenarian ideas in the north-east of Ireland, in an attempt to throw some light on when and how these have been expressed, and how they relate to the wider social and political context.

Although it has now evolved to embrace secular as well as religious matters, apocalyptic belief is of course merely an undercurrent in contemporary thought. Nonetheless, given both the evangelical and the divided nature of our society, it is not surprising that individuals and groups intermittently look to a cataclysmic end of time to resolve our difficulties. Northern Ireland is acknowledged to be a region whose people are more deeply influenced by religion than those in other parts of the United Kingdom or in the rest of Ireland.[12] With the language and symbols of millennial ideology deeply ingrained in our culture, a tradition with such longevity and adaptability has offered many a sense of hope in the midst of despair.

NOTES

1 REV. W.J. CHRISTIE, *The Time of the End* (Gortin, n.d.).
2 DAMIAN THOMPSON, *The End of Time: Faith and Fear in the Shadow of the Millennium* (London, Vintage, 1999 edition), p. 9.
3 J.F.C. HARRISON, *The Second Coming: Popular Millenarianism: 1780–1850* (London, Routledge and Kegan Paul, 1979), pp. 3–4.
4 DAVID and PAT ALEXANDER (eds), *The Lion Handbook to the Bible* (Berkhamstead, Lion Publishing, 1973).
5 JOHN D. BREWER with GARETH I. HIGGINS, *Anti-Catholicism in Northern Ireland, 1600–1998* (Basingstoke, Macmillan, 1998), pp. 148–9.
6 Ibid, p. 24.
7 W.H. OLIVER, *Prophets and Millennialists: The Uses of Biblical Prophecy in England from the 1790s to the 1840s* (Auckland, Oxford, Auckland University Press, 1978), p. 17.
8 Examples of numerological mysticism are everywhere within millennial writing, but see Thompson for a summary.
9 THOMPSON, *The End of Time*, p. 145.
10 *Joy Bells*, April, 1886.
11 MARINA BENJAMIN, *Living at the end of the World* (London, Picador, 1998), p. 65.
12 STEVE BRUCE, *Religion in Modern Britain* (Oxford, Oxford University Press, 1995), p. 60.

Oliver Cromwell
Courtesy of the Linen Hall Library

1

PLANTERS, PROPHETS AND PRESBYTERIANS

POST-REFORMATION IRELAND

This know also,
that in the last days perilous times shall come
2 Timothy 3: 1

MILLENNIAL IDEOLOGY has at least two major strands – the intellectual and the popular – and, as J.F.C. Harrison points out, the latter sprang from an emotional rather than an intellectual stimulus, and thus frequently lay outside the realms of conscious reasoning.[1] Linked to a more general belief in divine intervention in daily life, its manifestations were many and varied, with biblical prophecies hopelessly intertwined with folk wisdom, astrology and popular prophecies.[2] Raymond Gillespie, in his study of religious belief in sixteenth- and seventeenth-century Ireland, for example, draws attention to the part played by dreams and visions in the popular understanding of 'the way in which the world worked'. Both Protestant and Catholic culture, he suggests, could tap into a belief system within which prophecy was accepted as a reality which could be 'tailored to meet any situation'.[3]

Given the religious tensions of the post-Reformation period, and the new power structure resulting from the 'plantation' of the north-east, it was almost inevitable that those on either side of the religious divide would from time to time seek divine justification for their social, economic and political claims. Events such as the 1641 'massacre' thus took central place in Protestant mythology, and in subsequent years as religious and ethnic conflict continued to dominate Irish affairs, it was viewed as part of a more universal struggle between the forces of good and evil. On the Catholic side, capitalising on the fear of mass destruction and the despair following harvest failures, rebels drew on the prophecies of Patrick and Columkille to assert the inevitability of the Irish reconquest of their land from the invader, with Sir Phelim O'Neill at one stage cast as the deliverer.[4] Settlers similarly saw God's hand at work on their behalf. The dreadful events of 1641 could be interpreted as an example of divine punishment visited on a people overly tolerant of Catholicism:

> The iniquities of the English nation which were very great in this Kingdom were now full: heaven and earth seemed to conspire together for the punishment of them. God certainly declared his high indignation against them for their great sins ... and suffered the barbarous rebels to be instruments of mischief as the cruel executioners of his wrath against them.[5]

On the other hand, when the tide turned in favour of the settlers in 1642, Robert Cole from Fermanagh was only one of many who interpreted the signs as 'the good that God hath done his Israel'.[6] Such explanations for secular triumphs or tribulations do not of course amount to full-blown millenialism, but they do suggest the commonality of a mental framework which saw God's hand at work in everyday occurrences.

While such popular beliefs represented only one strand in a complex socio-political situation, in England during this period prophecy played a more central role, with political, military and religious affairs inextricably interwoven in the upheaval of civil war.[7] For many protagonists in the battle between king and parliament, the established institutions of church and state were identified alongside the Papacy as the forces of Antichrist, and separatists, believing that they were living in the last days, directed their own actions toward helping bring about the end of time.[8] Amongst the most radical, in both political and religious terms, were the Fifth Monarchy Men, who interpreted the execution of Charles I on 30 January 1649 as signalling the onset of Christ's Kingdom on earth, an event for which it was their duty to prepare.[9] There were many other, mostly short-lived sects, whose beliefs represented a real threat to the existing order. More established religious groups whose powerful sense of the approaching apocalyptic conversion of the world resulted in persecution in the mid-seventeenth century, but who would outlive the crisis, included Baptists and Quakers.[10]

This sense of impending apocalyptic change was perhaps most strongly seen in the actions of Cromwell's 'Bare Bones' parliament of 1653 which went so far as to pass a resolution looking forward to the return of Christ. For radical English thinkers of this era, there was no contradiction in the pursuit of 'liberty in place of tyranny, and ... godliness in place of idolatry';[11] they regarded the Monarchy as an evil to be eradicated, and Cromwell's army as 'that corner stone cut out of the mountain which must dash the earth to pieces'.[12] To such men, Ireland was more than just strategically important. Fear of invasion, heightened by the end of the Thirty Years' War in Europe in 1648, and the overwhelmingly Catholic nature of the neighbouring island, linked secular and religious preoccupations and ensured the identification of the Irish as part of the international forces of the 'Man of Sin'.[13] The Cromwellian army was thus envisaged as God's instrument for the final overthrow of the Antichrist.[14] Christopher Hill argues that the regiments which fought in Ireland were the most radical in the English army, avenging the massacre of 1641 and fighting 'with a savagery' such as had been recommended to those 'fighting against Antichrist'.[15] Indeed, a sermon preached before the House of Commons in December of the same year suggested a clear link between the two:

> Arise Oh Lord and scatter the Irish rebels
> Arise Oh Lord and confound the Antichrist.[16]

However, despite radical support for the conquest of Ireland, the proliferation of Puritan sects which had arisen during the religious and political turmoil in England made little headway here, with only the Baptists and Quakers establishing any significant presence. By 1653 Baptist congregations had been formed in Dublin, Wexford, Waterford, Clonmel, Cork, Kerry, Limerick, Galway and Carrickfergus, while Quakers gathered in Dublin, Cork and Waterford, and in rural areas.[17] Although Quakers were still frequently subjected to persecution, both sects had by this stage shed their more extreme millennial elements.[18] Radical individuals such as

John Rogers, who became a Fifth Monarchist on his return to England, did have an impact on religious life in Dublin where his congregation became a centre of Baptism, but there is no evidence of the more extreme sect taking root.[19] Muggletonians, who believed that the Two Last Witnesses foretold in Revelation 11 were of their number, caused only a brief flurry of disruption in religious circles in Cork.[20]

Patrick O'Farrell explains the absence of sect-type developments in this period by stressing both the embattled nature of Irish Catholicism and the Protestant ascendancy's fixation on its own vulnerable position.[21] Nonetheless, Toby Barnard suggests that the messianic Cromwellian campaign in Ireland was influential in shaping the attitudes of the English administration, particularly in terms of its anti-Catholicism; he quotes Colonel John Jones, a parliamentary commissioner in Dublin from 1650 to 1654, who believed that they had been led by God,

> into a strange land and to act in as strange a work, a work that neither we nor our forefathers knew or heard of: the framing or forming of a commonwealth out of a corrupt rude mass.[22]

Anti-Catholicism was a powerful force in both England and Ireland in this period, and the reputation of Archbishop Ussher, much admired for his 'firm anti-Catholicism' was deliberately fostered on both sides of the Irish Sea, with much made of his 'uncanny prophecy' of the 1641 massacre and the future trials of Protestantism.[23] As Raymond Gillespie points out, however, Ussher's reputation for prophecy was 'subtly advanced for him after his death in a carefully worded biography by his chaplain, Nicholas Bernard',[24] and there appears to have been little interest in prophetical matters amongst the Irish more generally. A group of visiting French prophets in the early eighteenth century had little success in their endeavour to convert Dubliners to their millennial perspective, finding their audiences as 'impenetrable as rocks',[25] and only a few examples of indigenous 'Holy Men' or visionaries have been recovered. Raymond Gillespie draws attention to Dubliner William Wright, who, late in life, wrote a chronology of the world, based on Revelation, which concluded that a child born in 1700 would live to see the last Pope in Rome.[26] A 1775 survey also uncovered two 'seekers of Inner Light': William Forde of Hercules Lane, Belfast, 'a poor man', living on roots and water, and in Carrickfergus:

> Edward Pendril, shoemaker, a married man who under great persecution lives in continence and abstinence from animal food ... He is tender-minded. He was with the Quakers but now fully believes in restitution, and the universality cf God's power and love.[27]

While such men could no doubt have a striking effect on individuals in their immediate community, they exerted no greater nor more lasting influence.

Amongst the various shades of Presbyterian opinion, which successfully made the transition from Scottish to Irish soil, apocalyptic ideas were probably strongest within the Covenanting tradition. While always numerically small in Ulster, this group's allegiance to the Solemn League and Covenant of 1643 and their continuing refusal to take political oaths resulted in intermittent persecution which only added to their sense of themselves as a chosen people entrusted with a divine mission.[28] One early Covenanting visitor to Ulster was itinerant preacher Alexander Peden whose sermons 'full of fire and flame' spread alarm through Armagh and Antrim in the 1680s, gaining him a reputation as a martyr and a prophet.[29]

Within mainstream Presbyterianism there appears to have been little interest in eschatology – the body of knowledge concerning the 'last things' or the end of the age – in this period, though the Rev. John Abernethy is a notable exception. Founder of the Belfast Society, a group of clergy and laymen dedicated to the advancement of religious knowledge, he preached a sermon to the Synod of Ulster in 1716 in which he predicted that that year would see the inauguration of the millennium. Abernethy would later became leader of a group, dubbed 'New Lights', who refused to subscribe to the Westminster Confession of Faith, and thus ensure his place in Irish Presbyterian history.[30]

Of course the language of millenialism could be used without any commitment to the belief that the end of the world was imminent. Barnard noted, for example, that during the 1720s Presbyterian preachers 'exploited the prophetic and providential modes' to encourage and inspire those of their people embarking on a new life across the Atlantic, telling them that 'God had appointed a country to them to dwell in (naming New England) and desires them to depart'.[31] For pilgrims and puritans from both Ireland and England, the prospect of building Christ's kingdom in the New World of the Americas was to prove a powerful draw.

Conditions in post-Reformation Ireland, however, were not really conducive to the maintenance of a sustained tradition of millennial ideologies; as Patrick O'Farrell puts it, 'the linkages necessary for a millennial movement between the world of rebellion and the world of religion did not exist'[32] – at least not until the closing decades of the eighteenth century when, for many, the world did indeed seem to 'turn upside down'.

NOTES

Thanks to John Lynch for providing helpful references as well as advice on this section.

1 J.F.C. HARRISON, *The Second Coming: Popular Millenarianism: 1780–1850* (London, Routledge and Kegan Paul, 1979).
2 DAMIAN THOMPSON, *The End of Time* (London, Vintage, 1999 ed.), p. 91.
3 RAYMOND GILLESPIE, *Devoted People: Belief and Religion in early Modern Ireland* (Manchester, Manchester University Press, 1997), pp. 127–47.
4 RAYMOND GILLESPIE, 'The end of an era: Ulster and the outbreak of the 1641 rising' in C. BRADY and R. GILLESPIE (eds), *Natives and Newcomers: Essays on the Making of Irish Colonial Society 1534–1641* (Dublin, Irish Academic Press, 1986), pp. 191–248, p. 210.
5 SIR JOHN TEMPLE, *History of the General Rebellion in Ireland* (Cork, 1766), pp. 97–8, quoted in GILLESPIE, *Devoted People*, pp. 54.
6 RAYMOND GILLESPIE, 'Destabilising Ulster, 1641–2' in BRIAN MACCURTA (ed.), *Ulster 1641* (Belfast, Institute of Irish Studies, 1993), pp. 107–121, p. 118.
7 CHRISTOPHER HILL, *Antichrist in Seventeenth-Century England* (Oxford, Oxford University Press, 1971), p. 155.
8 CHRISTOPHER HILL, *The World Turned Upside Down* (London, Maurice Temple Smith Ltd, 1972).
9 B.S. CAPP, *The Fifth Monarchy Men: A Study in Seventeenth-Century English Millenarianism* (Faber, 1972), p. 14.
10 HILLEEL SCHWARTZ, *The French Prophets: The History of a Millenarian Group in Eighteenth-Century England* (Berkeley, Los Angeles, University of California Press, 1980), p. 52.
11 Ibid., p. 13.

12 KEVIN A. CREED, 'The Pamphleteers' Protestant Champion: Viewing Oliver Cromwell through the Media of his Day', *Essays in History*, Vol. 34 (1992), pp. 19–39.
13 CHRISTOPHER HILL, 'Seventeenth-Century English Radicals and Ireland', in PATRICK CORISH (ed.), *Radicals, Rebels and Establishments* (Belfast, Appletree Press, 1985), pp. 33–49.
14 HILL, 'Seventeenth-Century English Radicals', p. 39.
15 HILL, *Antichrist in Seventeenth-Century England*, p. 174.
16 Ibid., p. 78.
17 PATRICK J. CORISH, 'The Cromwellian Regime, 1650–60', in T.W. MOODY, F.X. MARTIN and F.J. BYRNE (eds), *A New History of Ireland*, Vol. III, (Oxford, Oxford University Press, 1991), pp. 317–86, p. 380.
18 J.G. SIMMS, 'The restoration, 1660–85', in MOODY et al., *A New History of Ireland*, pp. 420–53, p. 438.
19 T.C. BARNARD, *Cromwellian Ireland: English Government and Reform in Ireland* 1649–1660 (Oxford, Oxford University Press, 1975), p. 105.
20 CHRISTOPHER HILL, BARRY REAY and WILLIAM LAMONT, *The World of the Muggletonians* (London, Maurice Temple Smith, 1983), pp. 55–6.
21 PATRICK O'FARRELL, 'Millennialism, Messianism and Utopianism in Irish History', *Anglo-Irish Studies*, ii (1976), pp. 45–68, pp. 48–50.
22 BARNARD, *Cromwellian Ireland*, p. 14.
23 Ibid, pp. 91–2.
24 RAYMOND GILLESPIE, *Devoted People*, p. 141.
25 SCHWARTZ, *The French Prophets*, pp. 154–5.
26 RAYMOND GILLESPIE, *Devoted People*, p. 141.
27 Quoted in HARRISON, *The Second Coming*, pp. 21–2.
28 MICHAEL DUREY describes the Covenantors as 'anti-authoritarian, and heavily impregnated with the doctrines of millenarianism', M. DUREY, *Transantlantic Radicals and the Early American Republic* (Kansas, University Press of Kansas, 1997), pp. 141–2.
29 PHIL KILROY, *Protestant Dissent and Controversy in Ireland, 1660–1714* (Cork, Cork University Press, 1994), pp. 116–8.
30 IAN MCBRIDE, *Scripture Politics: Ulster Presbyterianism and Irish Radicals in Late Eighteenth-Century Ireland* (Oxford, Clarendon, 1998), pp. 43–4.
31 TONY BARNARD, 'The Government and Irish Dissent, 1704–1880', in KEVIN HERLIHY (ed.), *The Politics of Irish Dissent 1650–1800* (Dublin, Four Courts Press, 1997), pp. 9–27, p. 18.
32 O'FARRELL, 'Millennialism, Messianism and Utopianism in Irish History', p. 47.

The Battle of Ballynahinch
Painting by Thomas Robinson
Courtesy of the Office of Public Works and the National Gallery, Dublin

2

RADICALS, REBELS AND REVIVALISTS

1798

This flame of freedom must precede,
Thy promised reign of grace:
The age millennial is decreed
But war's alarms must cease![1]

At the end of the eighteenth century apocalyptic beliefs could be found among Bavarian illuminati, Scandinavian Swedenborgians, Polish and Russian Occultists in St. Petersburg, Spanish Jesuits, American Shakers, New England Congregationalists, Seneca Indians, Appalachian Methodists, Welsh Baptists, and the more excitable Freemasons.[2]

IN IRELAND ALSO, the impact of revolution in both America and France was pervasive and profound. The belief that a new age was dawning and that institutions of 'tyranny' were about to collapse injected fervour and an unprecedented level of optimism into campaigns for political reform. At a time when new ideas were still largely mediated through religious belief, this new-found confidence in the inevitability of social and political progress was reinforced by a surge of interest in prophetical writings linking the contemporary situation with the onset of the millennium.[3] Thus American Puritans saw the 'Mark of the Beast' in the Stamp Act imposed by Britain, cast George I in the role of Antichrist and believed the War of Independence to be part of a prophetic plan to free God's people.

Elsewhere, identification of the Papacy as the Antichrist was by now common; as one contemporary put it, 'the Pope is that monster and Rome and its seven hills the seat of his delusions'.[4] The dramatic changes within the French Catholic church were thus central to most eschatological works, with the radical shift in the balance of power between Protestantism and Catholicism in Europe widely welcomed.[5] The situation was, of course, viewed as particularly significant on the island of Ireland, where political and religious relations at both local and national level were marked by religious differences. While the gradual relaxation of the penal laws during the eighteenth century was evidence of continuing reform, Catholics still suffered from a range of political and social inequalities, and during the 1790s the campaign for their liberties once again gathered momentum. In the revolutionary discourse of the Society of the United Irishmen, which claimed to unite Catholic, Protestant and Dissenter, religious and political ideologies were inextricably interwoven.

Another – and perhaps more ominous – context, however, was provided by localised outbreaks of sectarian violence in the southern border counties of Ulster, where economic and demographic factors proved a particularly volatile combination. By the end of the eighteenth century Armagh was not only one of the most populous counties in Ireland, but its population was made up of almost equal numbers of Protestants and Catholics. While this demographic equilibrium created the potential for sectarian conflict, further tension was generated as a result of industrial expansion in the area. In the first place, the rise of independent smallholders, directly employed by drapers or bleachers, caused a breakdown in traditional forms of social control, temporarily weakening the bond between Protestant gentry and Protestant weavers. Secondly, although Roman Catholics were latecomers to the weaving trade in the eighteenth century, the relaxation of the penal laws and the prosperity generated by the local linen industry put them in a position to compete in the land market and thus challenge traditional notions of ascendancy. The acquisition of arms by Catholics through the Volunteer movement and continuing radical demands for political concessions further eroded social stability in Armagh. This dangerous fusion of social, economic and political competition between the religious communities produced the conflicts fought out by the Catholic Defenders and the Protestant Peep O'Day Boys, with the formation of the Orange Order in 1795 creating a new and vibrant channel for the expression of Protestant identity.

This localised experience of bitterness, competition and confrontation contrasted strongly with the heady and idealistic rhetoric of the United Irishmen who believed they were entering

> a very advanced and enlightened period of the world, when ignorance and superstition are falling like lightning from Heaven, and knowledge is making very rapid strides.[6]

The fall of the Bastille, the symbol of the new age of liberty, was celebrated annually in Belfast on 14 July, and, from this centre of progressive Presbyterianism, men of the liberal middle class, who prided themselves on their political and religious radicalism, claimed rights for themselves and their fellow Catholic citizens. However, if demography was an important factor in determining religious relations in the south of the province, it was equally so in Belfast, this time in furthering a spirit of co-operation. For in the late eighteenth century, Catholics were few in number in this growing northern town; in 1785, for example, they accounted for only around 8% of the population, and therefore represented no threat to the Protestant way of life. Indeed munificent town-dwellers had expressed their liberality by contributing almost half the cost of the building of Belfast's first Roman Catholic chapel in 1784. It was thus from a position of relative security that many Presbyterian liberals saw in the revolutionary ardour of the 1790s the opportunity for securing political and religious equality with both their Episcopalian and Catholic neighbours.

While recent studies have stressed that political radicalism was by no means the most dominant feature of Ulster Presbyterianism,[7] the involvement of several clergy in the Society of the United Irishmen was highly significant. The views of ministers such as Samuel Barber, Thomas Ledlie Birch and William Steel Dickson, for example, were disseminated through pulpit and press and made an important contribution to the revolutionary ardour of the times. Inspired by the belief that 'biblical revelation and enlightenment rationalism were not only compatible, but also intimately related',[8] these men drew deeply on the tradition of biblical prophecy in their interpretation of events in America, France and Ireland. Though their expositions of the Books of Daniel and Revelation often differed in exact details, they were united in their view that God was hastening the downfall of Popery and Prelacy.

In June 1791, in a sermon preached to the Synod of Ulster, Barber welcomed the spirit of enlightenment:

> Rejoice at the amazing advance of knowledge and the progress of science which must ever be favourable to truth and fatal to error. Science enlarges the mind, ascertains the Rights of Man and before science sooner or later all tyranny must fall.[9]

While he believed that the gradual way in which the Antichrist had risen to power made precise predictions difficult, Barber was clearly of the view that the 'mighty conquest' over 'superstition, idolatry and religious slavery' was soon to be accomplished. Like many of his Presbyterian colleagues, Barber included *all* religious establishments in his definition of tyranny, and though Thomas Ledlie Birch followed a more orthodox line, he would later make the same point:

> By the name Antichrist we do not imagine, that not any man, or class of men, is designed in scripture, but a system now known in the world (particularly under the name of church establishment) planned and carried on, under various agencies, which (as occasion served) has persecuted all religions, and opposed all reformation.[10]

In his address to the Synod on the theme of 'The Obligations upon Christians and Especially Ministers to be Exemplary in their Lives' in 1794, Birch brought a powerful sense of urgency to his appeal by a close interpretation of the scriptures which concluded that Christ's return was imminent:

> We must think that the final overthrow of the Beast, or the opposing power, is almost at the door; and especially as we may observe in a certain contest the seemingly literal accomplishment of the Battle of Armageddon, in which the Beast and his adherents are to be cut off, as a prelude to the peaceful reign of 1,000 years.[11]

As early as 1777 William Steel Dickson had also preached on the advisability of living one's life in a state of readiness for the second coming,[12] and by the end of the century the text, 'Be ye, therefore, ready also, for the Son of Man cometh, at an hour, when ye think not', had become almost overworked. In *Three Sermons on Scripture Politics* delivered in the early 1790s, Dickson also outlined the history of abuses of power by churchmen, attacked the injustices suffered by Irish Catholics, and looked forward to brighter times. The French experience offered both an example and a warning:

> [This] great and enlightened nation has burst the chains of prejudice and slavery, disclaimed the idea of conquest for dominion, opened the temple of liberty for all religious denominations at home, and sent forth her arms, *not to destroy*, but *restore* the liberty of the world, and extend her blessings to all who dare, and by daring, deserve to be free. Tyrants already tremble at her name, while oppressed nations exult in her success, receive her sons with gratitude and joy, and unite in her cause. Happy! Thrice happy the people, whose rulers may become wise, by the lesson which she has been obliged to write in letters of blood.– Where the ear of the prince may be open to the voice of humanity reciting her grievances, and supplicating redress, and the necessity and horrors of revolution precluded by *seasonable* and *radical* reform! That this may be our case is the prayer of my heart.[13]

All three of these Presbyterian millenialists had acquired reputations for political radicalism. Barber had founded one of the first United Irish Societies in his Rathfriland congregation; Birch was to be arrested and sent into exile in western Pennsylvania, where he and his new congregation 'attempted to build a Christian Republican community that would prepare itself for the Second Coming'.[14] William Steel Dickson, adjutant general of the County Down United Irishmen, was considered 'one of the most active and persevering of the rebel traitors in promoting the system of the United Irishmen and the Rebellion'.[15] While their theological views covered a broad range, all three ministers were members of the General Synod of Ulster, which sought to dissociate itself from their political activism, regretting the actions of 'these few unworthy members of our Body, whose conduct we can only view with grief and indignations'.[16] But although they were in a minority, there is no doubt that the leadership role of Presbyterian ministers was a significant factor in the growth of the United Irish movement in the north: a total of thirty ministers and eighteen probationers from the different branches of Presbyterianism were implicated in the disturbances.

We have already noted the millennial predisposition within the

Covenanting tradition, and both David Miller and Peter Brooke have seen the readiness of Irish Covenanting ministers to identify the government alongside the Papacy as a force of Antichrist, as another important factor in the rise of United Irish support in the Presbyterian north-east. For these men too, 'the simplified confrontation between the forces of Christ and Antichrist was confused with the equally simplified confrontation promoted by the United Irishmen between the forces of liberty and the forces of despotism'.[17] The Rev. James McKinney of Dervock, County Antrim, was forced to flee to America in 1793 following accusations of publishing sedition in a sermon which proclaimed that

> the signs of the times call upon all who have any interest to employ it with God that he would hasten the downfall of Popery, Prelacy, Judaism, together with Mahometan delusion ...[18]

Rousing sermons by Covenanting preacher, the Rev. William Gibson of Kells, County Antrim were also widely circulated at this time. According to one contemporary source, in services lasting up to six hours, Gibson

> at times, so far forgot himself as to relapse into his holy hatred of popery by introducing the antiquated dogmas of his sect in allusions to the 'man of sin', and to an old jade dressed in scarlet, dyed with the blood of the saints, said to reside near Babylon.[19]

The sermons of William Staveley, whose itinerancy resulted in the establishment of five Covenanting congregations, were also regarded as highly dangerous to the political establishment. Stressing that 'no man, no matter how great or powerful, whatever his station in life', could escape God's judgement, Staveley encouraged his fellow 'watchmen upon Zion's walls' to

> joyfully wait the happy day, now fast coming on, when Babylon's fall in the east, and through all Europe, will be announced by an angel's trumpet; then will the conqueror's song be sweetly sung by all his victorious army.[20]

Other writers were even more direct in their challenge to the existing social order; a 1793 tract published in Strabane, for example, claimed that

> The courts of kings, the seats and palaces of noblemen, the banqueting houses of the luxurious, the full barns of farmers, the cottages of husbandmen, and the stalls under which beggars lie, will be as one and come to nothing.[21]

It is perhaps not surprising that the political and social implications of such rhetoric were viewed with alarm in official circles.

The year 1795 was particularly prolific in terms of millennial publications, some of which were reprints from the English civil war of the previous century. The titles reflect the perceived relevance of biblical prophecy in a time of crisis and include, for example, John Owen, *The Shaking and Translation of Heaven and Earth* (Belfast); James Bicheno, *The Signs of the Times* (Belfast); Robert Fleming, *A Discourse on the Rise and Fall of Antichrist, wherein the Revolution in France and the Downfall of the Monarchy in that Kingdom are Distinctly Pointed Out* (Belfast); *Extracts from the Prophecies of Richard Brothers* (Belfast) and *Prophetical Extracts particularly such as relate to the Revolution in France* (Strabane).[22]

The *Northern Star*, 'the first and most significant newspaper' of the United Irishmen, was also not above making use of prophecies old and new 'to appeal to the cruder beliefs of the lower orders' and exploit the apocalyptic mood in the countryside in promotion of their political cause.[23] The following 'Queries', for example, were contributed by 'A Believer in Prophecy' (possibly Birch) on 24 April 1793:

> Querie I. In what period was to take place, the fall of Antichrist, or the two beasts spoken of in the Revelation, (termed in the original, Wild Beasts) which by comparing Revelation with David 7th chap. and 17 the verse, appears to signify Tyranny in the Christian and Mahomentan World?
>
> Querie II. Has the present contest in which the World is about to be engaged, any of the striking features of the battle in which the beast and his party were to be totally overthrown, as a prelude to the flowing in of Jew and Gentile into the Christian Church: and an introduction to the peaceful reign of a thousand years? – described in Revelations, chapter 12, from the 11th verse.
>
> Querie III. Is it not a matter of the first importance, seriously to weigh these particulars, least they should, unawares, fall under the

> weighty stroke of the sword of him that sitteth upon a white horse, and maketh war in righteousness.[24]

The power of print thus played an important role in the politicisation of popular culture, particularly in east Ulster which had a high level of literacy.[25] As one government official complained,

> Unless you see that infernal paper, you can have no idea of the length to which it goes, of the innumerable falsehoods which it circulates among the credulous populace, of the style of its paragraphs, exquisitely adapted to the tastes and understanding of the northerners, of the ability, in short, with which it is conducted. … The lowest of the people get it. It is read to them in clusters. A whole neighbourhood will subscribe for it.[26]

The United Irishmen also appointed local people to read and explain the old prophecies of Thomas the Rhymer and Alexander Peden, and to 'tell the French news to everybody and dispute with all who dare to contradict them'.[27] Contemporary historian, Samuel McSkimin reported that such activities promoted 'confidence and enthusiasm among the ignorant', and in areas where religious tensions were high, had a very different effect from those desired by the United Irishmen. One stirring example had 'an angel reading out of a green book the order for the extirpation of the English interest in Ireland', and Roman Catholics were seriously alarmed by a contemporary version of the prophecies of St Columbkille which suggested their imminent massacre

> by a murderous band called the black militia, which was always construed to mean the Orangemen. … Reports were also spread in the Glyns, county of Antrim and other Roman Catholic districts, that the Orangemen were coming at night to massacre them in their beds, having entered into a compact to wade knee deep in their blood. [28]

Although, as an opponent of the United Irishmen, McSkimin would have been keen to emphasise sectarian tensions, such prophecies must have seemed particularly plausible during 1795–6, when around 7,000 Catholics were driven from their Armagh homes in a two-month period.[29] At the same time, the spread of the secret, violent, Defender organisation, and rumours of French involvement, the granting of new political rights to Roman Catholics (a Catholic

Enfranchisement Act was passed in 1793) and the disbandment of the Volunteers led many Protestants to lose confidence in state institutions, and united landlords and tenants in the specifically Protestant, anti-Catholic Orange movement. Each of these opposing groups drew deeply on religious traditions to assert both their righteousness and their certainty of success. Freemasonry provided a clear model for secret societies of the time, and the Defenders' catechisms reflect its mysticism and symbolism, the language rich in biblical imagery:

> Who is your father? God. Who is your mother? The true Catholic Church. Who is your brother? The second person of the Holy Trinity. What order are you from? From the order of St Patrick. Where do you stand? I stand upon the rock that St Peter built the church on. The gates are open, they are. How many? Twelve. For whom? The children of Abraham. Where? In Paradise. Is this a cloak you wear? No, but a mantle. How did you become to wear a mantle? Because I succeeded Elizah and Elizah succeeded Joshua and Joshua begat Moses and I begat to wear a mantle.[30]

It was statements such as these which so alarmed local Protestants, whose fears were intensified in the 1790s by the belief that the Defenders would be actively assisted by the French. Local events contributed to an anxious sense of persecution; Lord Charlemont received an alarming report from Ballymena in 1797:

> We are like Christians in the first century, who every day expected the world would be at an end, and in contemplation of that great event, every idea was absorbed. So here, nothing can persuade us but that some great event is at hand (invasion, massacre). God grant it may be otherwise ...[31]

During years when murder and looting were commonplace, secret societies proliferated, a repressive military presence was established, and the daily newspapers were full of the dramatic occurrences in France and the progress of the war, such references to the imminence of the Latter Days abounded at both popular and intellectual levels.

Whether construed as an academic theological exercise, or, more commonly, expressed in the general linking of contemporary social upheaval with the unfolding of a divine plan for mankind, the scriptural interpretation of political events did come to have a directly spiritual as opposed to purely political significance, particularly after the disillusionment of the late 1790s. The Christian system of rewards and punishments acquired immediacy and a new significance in a context of social convulsion and apocalyptic expectancy amongst a people 'who had not yet felt the full impact of modernisation', and who retained the propensity to view human affairs as subject to divine intervention.[32] Such expectancy transcended the fears and problems of everyday life, and was an important inducement to religious commitment. For many of evangelical faith, for whom 'moderation and gradualness did not commend themselves as virtues, but rather were signs of a lack of faith',[33] political and social events were translated into signs of the imminent arrival of the Messiah and the Last Judgement, investing all aspects of life with a compelling urgency. Such an atmosphere particularly benefited those sects whose preaching approximated the intensity of the situation.

The Methodist movement, for example, expanded dramatically in south Ulster in this period, mostly as a result of local revivals. Charismatic preacher Gideon Ouseley, writing in the winter of 1799, described the drama and emotion of his mission:

> On Monday we came to Bailieborough. The market-people were assembled when we came into the street. We did not alight, but prepared immediately to attack the devil's kingdom which still remained strong in this town. The Methodists wished us out of the street, when they saw the manner of our proceedings, riding on our horses, with our umbrellas over our heads, the day being wet, but a young girl was so alarmed that she feared the day of judgment was at hand.[34]

For preachers and religious leaders, the spirit of revival, which was being manifest throughout the countryside, was in itself a further indication of the coming Glory of God. Thomas Coke, President of the British Methodist movement, wrote to an American Preacher of his hopes that Ireland would partake of the revivalistic fervour that had swept America:

> Surely, you cannot be mistaken in the signs of the times. The Lord is hastening apace the great Millennium, when Christ shall reign with his ancients gloriously a thousand years … ! One of the most sure signs of the approach of the Millennium will be the having a multitude of real possessors of that mighty blessing on our society.[35]

Birch, writing in 1799, described a similar optimism:

> The people of Europe and especially Ireland, are inspired with a well-grounded belief and hope that the time is arrived when the prophecies concerning the universal dominion of Christ's Kingdom, and the peaceful happy state upon earth, that is thereupon to ensue, or set forth … are to be fulfilled.[36]

The belief that 'the papal anti-Christ would soon fall in France and that Christianity would be brought to the heathen and the Jew in preparation for Christ's Second Coming' encouraged a proliferation of missionary initiatives on both sides of the Irish Sea.[37] The Evangelical Society of Ulster was founded in 1798 in direct response to the political crisis; its new secretary explained the impulse behind the new initiative:

> To be found at any time slumbering upon Zion's walls, is very inconsistent with the character of a faithful watch-man; but in times like the present, it must be peculiarly so. Never surely, was there a more eventful period than this, in which our lot has been cast. What lover of the Gospel, who that ever prays in sincerity, 'Thy Kingdom come,' we ask, what soldier of the cross, can stand neuter at present, or remain at ease in Zion?[38]

Francis Dobbs

In the aftermath of rebellion, when it did indeed seem that things would never be the same again, the Union debates perpetuated popular excitement and unrest. Few, however, could link the political and religious principles with such ingenuous simplicity as Francis Dobbs, MP for Charlemont, whose interpretations of both biblical and daily events enlivened the House of Commons in the first summer of the nineteenth century. Dobbs saw the immediate Second Coming as inevitable, given the attempt to unite Ireland with Britain, since he believed her independence was 'written in the immutable records of Heaven'. He identified Armagh with Armageddon and viewed the proposed union as an attempt to annihilate God's chosen nation. On debating the issue, he thus assured his parliamentary colleagues that

> ... feeling as I do, that we are not living in ordinary times – feeling as I do, that we are living in the most momentous and eventful period of the world – feeling as I do, that a new and better order of things is about to arise, and that Ireland, in that new order of things, is to be highly distinguished indeed, this bill has no terrors for me. [39]

Nor would he despair if, somehow, the bill should pass into law; in that case he would

> ... submit to it without a murmur until it be repealed, or until the Sun shall miraculously withhold its light and announce the appearance of Christ. Should this bill receive the Royal Assent, I mean to inculcate into the minds of all who are sprung from me, or over whom I have the least influence, to pay it the most implicit obedience, till the MESSIAH shall in person demand their allegiance. – Acting under the strong conviction that I feel of this certainty ... I say to every man within and without these walls, whether he be a Christian or not, if he sincerely loves his fellow-creature, let him rejoice, for that MESSIAH who suffered on the cross is now about to accomplish all the objects of his mission. He is now about to take away the curse that followed the fall of Adam, and to renovate the earth. He is now about to establish a kingdom founded in justice, in truth, and in righteousness, that shall extend from pole to pole, and which shall place this hitherto wicked and miserable world upon the highest pinnacle of human happiness and human glory.[40]

While it is easy to view 'Millennium Dobbs' as a particularly quaint eccentric, contemporaries were aware of his popularity, particularly amongst the 'lower orders'. Moreover, his links to United Irish leader Thomas Russell remind us of the pervasive nature of millennial views amongst a wide range of political and religious thinkers. The subject of the famous recitation 'The Man from God-knows-where', Russell survived the events of '98 only to be hanged in Downpatrick gaol for his part in Robert Emmet's 'Cabbage patch rebellion' six years later. In his appeal for a stay of execution, Russell explained that he wished to complete a 'work of some advantage to the world', based on the Revelations of St John and on the writings of Francis Dobbs.[41] In an earlier *Letter to the People of Ireland on the present situation of the country*, he demonstrated a heavy reliance on theology, warning his readers of

> That great and dreadful day when all the human race shall appear in

> the presence of their creator and judge: when the heavens and earth shall fly away from his face and the guilty shall in vain call upon the rocks and mountains to hide and cover them: when the innocent blood which had been shed shall be avenged, what answer could be made?[42]

The writings of Dobbs and Russell, providing further evidence of the radical nature and potent force of millennial expectations, also provide intriguing examples of an Anglican strand of millenialism.

Millennial ideology during this period was complex, diverse and adaptable. For those with a vested interest in the world changing quickly it was possible to construct an optimistic eschatology in which temporal events were interpreted as the ushering in of a new and a better age. For those with most to lose from rapid social change, however, the reverse was the case, though for them divine providence was still regarded as incomparably superior to temporal misfortunes. In addition, for those whose view of the last times incorporated a post-millennial emphasis on a new 'gospel age' before the final curtain descended on the world, eschatological excitement could inspire a new enthusiasm for evangelism. All three strands were evident in the millenarian enthusiasm of late eighteenth-century Ulster.

NOTES

1 PINDARICUS, 'Ode to the New Year', *Northern Star*, 11 January 1792. Thanks to John Gray for this reference.
2 Quoted in DAMIAN THOMPSON, *The End of Time* (London, Vintage, 1999 ed.), p. 112.
3 D.N. HEMPTON, 'Evangelicalism and Eschatology', *Journal of Ecclesiastical History*, Vol. 31, No. 2, (1980), pp. 179–194.
4 SAMUEL BARBER, manuscript sermon preached before the General Synod of Ulster, Presbyterian Historical Society, Church House, Belfast.
5 PETER BROOKE, *Ulster Presbyterianism: the Historical Perspective, 1610–1970* (Belfast, Gill and Macmillan, 1994), pp. 104–5.
6 THOMAS LEDLIE BIRCH, *A Letter from an Irish Emigrant to his Friend in the United States* (Philadelphia, 1799).
7 MYRTLE HILL, 'The Religious Context: Protestantism in County Down in 1798' in M. HILL, B. TURNER & K. DAWSON (eds), *1798: Rebellion in County Down* (Newtownards, Colourpoint, 1998), pp. 6–77.

8 IAN MCBRIDE, 'When Ulster joined Ireland: Anti-Popery, Presbyterian Radicalism and Irish Republicanism in the 1790s', *Past and Present*, 157, pp. 63–93, p. 68.
9 BARBER, ms. Sermon.
10 T.L. BIRCH, *Seemingly Experimental Religion* (Washington, 1806), pp. 15–16.
11 Amongst a collection of unpublished manuscript sermons, PHS, Church House, Belfast.
12 W.S. DICKSON, *Sermon on the Coming of the Son of Man preached before the Particular Synod of Belfast, at their annual meeting, Nov. 4, 1777, Belfast* (Belfast, 1777).
13 WILLIAM STEELE DICKSON, *Three Sermons on Scripture Politics, Christmas Day* (1792). Pamphlets and sermons can be found at the Linen Hall Library, Belfast.
14 DAVID WILSON, *United Irishmen, United States: Immigrant Radicals in the Early Republic* (Dublin, Four Courts Press, 1998), p. 122.
15 Quoted in, W.D. BAILEY, 'Presbyterian Clergymen and the County Down rebellion of 1798', in HILL, TURNER and DAWSON, *1798: Rebellion in County Down*, pp. 162–86, p. 163.
16 *Records of the General Synod of Ulster, 1691–1820*, Volume 3 (Belfast, 1898), pp. 208–9.
17 D. MILLER, 'Presbyterianism and Modernisation in Ulster', *Past and Present* (1980), pp. 68–90; PETER BROOKE, 'Controversies in Ulster Presbyterianism, 1790–1836' (Unpublished Ph.D. thesis, Cambridge University, 1981), p. 35.
18 JAMES MCKINNEY, *Causes of Fasting* (1792).
19 SAMUEL MCSKIMIN, *Annals of Ulster: from 1790 to 1798* (Belfast, B.J. Cleeland, 1906), p. 54.
20 WILLIAM STAVELEY, *War Proclaimed and Victory Ensured* (Belfast, 1795).
21 KEVIN WHELAN, 'An Underground Gentry? Catholic Middlemen in Eighteenth-Century Ireland' in JAMES S. DONNELLY Jr. and KERBY A. MILLER (eds), *Irish Popular Culture 1650–1850* (Dublin, Irish Academic Press, 1998), pp. 118–72, p. 155.
22 J.R.R. ADAMS, *The Printed Word and the Common Man: Popular Culture in Ulster 1700–1900* (Belfast, Institute of Irish Studies, 1987), p. 89.
23 M. DUREY, *Transantlantic Radicals and the Early American Republic* (Kansas, University of Kansas Press, 1997), p. 117.
24 *Northern Star* (November, 1793).
25 KEVIN WHELAN, *The Tree of Liberty: Radicalism, Catholicism and the Construction of the Irish Identity 1760–1830* (Cork, Cork University Press in assoc. with Field Day, 1996).
26 JOHN SCHOALES, 1797, quoted in JOHN GRAY, 'Northern Star: that Infernal Paper', *Causeway: Cultural Traditions Journal* (Winter, 1997), pp. 22–4.
27 MCSKIMIN, *Annals*, pp. 49-50.
28 Ibid., p. 99.
29 JONATHAN BARDON, *A History of Ulster* (Belfast, Blackstaff Press, 1992), pp. 226–7.
30 THOMAS BARTLETT, 'Select Documents XXXVIII: Defenders and Defenderism in 1795' in *Irish Historical Studies*, Vol. XXIV, No. 95 (May, 1985), pp. 373–394, p. 389.
31 *The Mss and Correspondence of James, 1st Earl of Charlemont*, Historical Mss Commission (London, 1891–4), 2 volumes, p. 303.
32 MILLER, 'Presbyterianism and Modernisation', p. 80.

33 J.F.C. HARRISON, *The Second Coming: Popular Millenarianism: 1780–1850* (London, Routledge and Kegan Paul, 1979), p. 6.
34 Ouseley Collection, viii, folio 10, Public Record Office of Northern Ireland.
35 Methodist Archive Research Centre, Manchester, PLP28.7.4.
36 T.L. BIRCH, *Sermon preached before the Very Reverend, the General Synod of Ulster, Lurgan, June 26, 1793* (Belfast, 1793).
37 ROGER H. MARTIN, 'The Place of the London Missionary Society in the Ecumenical Movement', *Journal of Ecclesiastical History*, Vol. 31, No. 3(July, 1980), pp. 283–300, p. 285.
38 GEORGE HAMILTON, *Introductory Memorial Respecting the Establishment and First Attempt of the Evangelical Society of Ulster, 10 October 1798* (Armagh, 1798).
39 Speech to House of Commons, 7th June 1800, in *Memoirs of Francis Dobbs, also Genuine Reports of his speeches in Parliament on the subject of an union, and his Prediction of the Second Coming of the Messiah* ... (Dublin, 1800), p. 35.
40 Ibid, pp. 46–7.
41 JOHN GRAY, 'Millennial Vision: Thomas Russell Re-assessed' in *Linen Hall Review*, vol. 6, no. 1 (Spring, 1989), pp. 5–9, p. 9.
42 Quoted in ibid, p. 8.

The Itinerant Preacher
Painting by Nathaniel Grogan
Provenance unknown

3

CRUSADERS AND CONTROVERSIES

THE 19TH CENTURY

But the day of the Lord will come as a thief in the night; in the which the heavens shall pass away with a great noise, and the elements shall melt with fervent heat, the earth also and the works that are therein shall be burned up. Seeing then that all these things shall be dissolved, what manner of persons ought ye to be in all holy conversation and godliness, looking for and hasting unto the coming of the day of God?

2 Peter 3: 10–12

THERE IS CONSIDERABLE DEBATE amongst Irish historians about the extent of millennial input into the various social and political upheavals of the nineteenth century. Clearly, however, it was neither completely absent nor lacking impact at local, if not national level. One such example within rural Catholicism was during the Rockite movement of the 1820s. Although Patrick O'Farrell suggests that prophecy played 'no more than a passive and supportive role' in agrarian protest,[1] J.S. Donnelly argues that in this instance 'millennial vision' went hand in hand with more specific local grievances, helping to rally rural Catholics on the side of the agitators. In the context of the Second Reformation movement – an evangelical campaign to convert the Catholics of Ireland – poor harvests, tithe wars and the growth of Orangeism, Donnelly makes a convincing case for a version of rural millenarianism, which had as both its justification and its rallying cry the hope of 'the obliteration of Protestant heresy, and by extension, the destruction of the Protestant Church and State in Ireland'.[2] This discourse was mostly based on the prophecies of Pastorini, written in 1790 and predicting the downfall of Protestantism in 1821–25. A source of considerable embarrassment to the Catholic hierarchy, Pastorini was reported to be a household name in the south in 1822–23, especially in the Limerick area. Within a few years, however, as Sean Connolly notes, the

> Catholic Emancipation campaign became the focus for many of the same resentments that had earlier found expression in agrarian violence as well as for the mood of millenarian expectation that shortly before had made Pastorini a household name.[3]

For those within the Protestant tradition, the early nineteenth century seemed full or foreboding, for while the failure of the United Irishmen was complete, the sectarian nature of the rebellion in south-east Ireland left the minority religious community with an anxious understanding of its vulnerability in a predominantly Catholic nation. The passage of Catholic Emancipation was only the first of a series of attacks on Protestant privilege, which were opposed with all the fervour of a scripture-based evangelical tradition. This pessimistic temporal context could, however, provide the spur for pre-millenialist ideology; that the Second Coming would precede the fall of Antichrist explained the continuing prosperity of Catholicism both in Ireland and elsewhere. Evangelicals, at this period strongly anti-Catholic, could thus interpret day-to-day events – local, national and international – as part of the process of prophetic fulfilment. For those who had much to lose from the political and religious challenges of their generation, the biblical promise of eventual victory was particularly appealing, and in Ulster both the Earl of Roden and the Duke of Manchester kept a wary eye on the Book of Revelation and the 'Signs of the Times'. From the midst of strife and unrest in County Cavan, William Krause, moral agent to the evangelical Lord Farnham, wrote:

> I firmly believe that the day of the Lord's Coming is not far off. I

> believe that the restless, dissatisfied spirit, which is abroad, is rapidly maturing that distress of nations and perplexity, which we are taught to consider as a forerunner of that day. I believe that the infidel, popish and every other abomination will gather daily strength to the day of battle.[4]

Krause's work on Lord Farnham's estate brought him into the very heart of the proselytising controversy of the so-called 'Second Reformation' movement. Appointed in 1840 to the Bethesda Chapel in Dublin, his lectures and sermons distinguished him as an ardent evangelical. As David Hempton points out, the premillenialism of men such as these served to stiffen evangelical anti-Catholicism and helps explain, for example, the intensity of later opposition to government funding for the training of Catholic priests at Maynooth.[5] Intense theological debate in this period also produced the Irvingite and the Plymouth Brethren movements which had a negative and disruptive impact on the established religion in particular.[6] The Plymouth Brethren evolved from a Dublin meeting led by ex-Anglican J.N. Darby, who moved to Plymouth in 1830, attracting significant numbers of evangelicals into a movement which focused particular attention on biblical prophecy. Irving would be more closely associated with the rise of the Catholic Apostolic church. Darby's interpretation of Revelations was based on the belief of a two-stage Advent:

> First, there would be a quiet appearance – the 'presence' of Christ, when all true Christians, the true church, would be removed from the earth. This was the 'rapture of the saints'. Only then, when the restraining presence of the Holy Spirit in His own people had been removed from the world scene, would the Antichrist arrive. His rule would be brought to an end by the second stage of the Advent – the public 'appearing' of Christ in glory.[7]

This interpretation, which appeared to reconcile some of the contradictions of the biblical prophecies, retained a sense of imminent expectation, with the 'true believers' keeping themselves separate from the world, in a constant state of readiness for their rapturous reward.

Although Brethrenism did not really 'take off' in the north of Ireland for another twenty years, prophetical conferences held at Albury Park, Surrey and at Powerscourt in County Wicklow, helped to spread these ideas and to generate excitement in the religious community. A perusal of the Church of Ireland press during this period reveals a range of opinions about the validity and value of such eschatological enquiry. One line of thought clearly expressed in the *Christian Examiner* was that it was the Christian's 'privilege and our duty to enquire';[8] that an 'animating belief in prophecy [was] one of the chief marks of a converted mind',[9] and that if such study could 'excite our diligent search of the Word, it has a promised blessing'.[10] Others, however, were more wary of the possible consequences of encouraging such 'speculation', pointing to the 'injurious character' of prophetical meetings; with large numbers of different kinds of people intent on reaching hasty conclusions in an atmosphere of excitement.[11] Commenting on the annual meetings held at the home of the pious Lady Powerscourt, for example, one contributor was concerned that 'the important questions connected with Millenarian topics are assumed, rather than proposed as debatable'. He went on to point to the 'wild and heretical notions connected too frequently with this dogma', but appeared particularly concerned with the gender and age group of the participants, declaring that he

> would certainly not select a miscellaneous assemblage, of which females and young persons form a large proportion, to propound many of the opinions we have heard were broached at the late meeting.[12]

That females were particularly susceptible to emotional and erroneous preaching was a common theme in eighteenth- and nineteenth-century religious discourse.

Anxieties were also expressed about the dangers of internal division caused by Irving and Darby, but a 'Connaught Curate' raised more fundamental worries about whether 'some of the Church of Ireland clergy who have entered fully into belief in the millennium [were] close to 'Romanists', with their references to purgatory, miracles, an infallible tribunal and the sacrifice of the mass'.[13] The conversion of Lady Powerscourt to Brethrenism, despite the best efforts of the local rector, eventually brought an end to the controversial meetings in her family home.[14]

While it is unlikely that these theological arguments had much effect on society at large, this is not to say that those lower down the social scale did not also ponder the close proximity of the next world. As contemporary sermon titles indicate, outbreaks of cholera, fever or famine could equally serve as an incentive to prepare for divine judgement: 'Pestilences arrested by Prayer', 'Blessed Turf v Cholera' and 'God's Judgment Considered', all dated 1832, suggest a more pragmatic approach to the Christian message. A Methodist preacher wrote from Donaghadee in the same period that,

> pressed by the messenger of death, and unknowing who next might be summoned to the cholera house or the grave, a general concern for eternal life pervaded the community.[15]

The Great Famine of the 1840s was of course the most serious disaster of the century, an 'event of cosmic significance' during which superstition and fear were rife; as one historian comments:

> The initial Catholic folk interpretation of the Famine was in terms of supernatural judgment. Studies of Irish folk tradition have shown that the commonplace reaction was to interpret the Famine as some form of divine punishment by the Christian God for the people's sins.[16]

Practical responses to the catastrophe, whether by government or philanthropists were heavily influenced by 'the twin doctrines of political economy and providentialism'.[17] Sir Charles Trevelyan, permanent head of the Treasury, was of the opinion that the Famine was

> ... the judgment of God on an indolent and unself-reliant people, and as God has sent the calamity to teach the Irish a lesson, that calamity must not be too much mitigated: the selfish and indolent must learn their lesson so that a new and improved state of affairs must arise.[18]

Studies in folklore suggest that a similar approach prevailed amongst the peasantry themselves. Some of them believed the famine was 'a visitation from God in punishment for waste' during the previous year's harvest, a view of divine wrath which the church apparently often encouraged: 'A priest told the people that this black pestilence was ruination from the hand of God'.[19]

Those commentators with specific political agendas, however, felt that earthly conditions were also responsible for Ireland's troubles. Daniel O'Connell thought it a 'visitation of Providence' for which the Government was to blame, and John Mitchel, of the revolutionary Young Ireland organisation, argued that 'The Almighty, indeed, sent the potato blight, but the English created the Famine'.[20] However, as Michael Barkun explains, such views did not evolve into millenarian expectancy or activity at either the popular or intellectual level, because

> ... the possibility of emigration served to empty the country of many of the most discontented and, presumably, the most able. Second, an unusually strong church may have provided an explanatory framework, which even a catastrophe of this magnitude could not erode. Finally, those who survived did so at the very margin of physical existence, and it may well be that we see at work here the familiar principle that 'when people toil from sunrise to sunset for a bare living, they nurse no grievances and dream no dreams'.[21]

While Protestant relief work was often genuinely altruistic in intention, for some evangelists the crisis provided an opportunity to step up their campaign to free the Catholic peasantry from popish influence and 'priestly tyranny'. Famine on Achill Island in 1831 had inspired Irish-speaking evangelical, the Rev. Edward Nangle, to establish a Protestant settlement there, aiming at the teaching and conversion of the Catholic population. A school which attracted 420 children within a year and with a printing press dedicated to attacks on 'the idolatry of the Roman Mass', made Nangle's settlement a focal point for evangelical visitors and, during the famine of the 1840s, a target for accusations of 'souperism' – the use of bribery to win converts.[22] While historian Desmond Bowen argues that local people undoubtedly gained in material terms from this experiment, the context of Nangle's work was clearly set out in the sub-title of the *Achill Missionary Herald*:

> A Monthly Journal, exhibiting the Principles and Progress of Christ's Kingdom, and exposing the Errors and Abominations of that section of the Rival Kingdom of Antichrist, commonly called THE PAPACY: together with a practical exposure of the Civil, Social, and Political delinquencies of the Pope's emissaries in attempting to establish his wicked usurpation throughout the world generally, AND ESPECIALLY IN THIS KINGDOM.[23]

The Herald regularly published articles on prophecy and the Antichrist, with Nangle, like many of his contemporaries, particularly excited by the rise to power of Napoleon III in the 1850s. This

'Napoleonism' was based on the belief that

> The dynasty founded by NAPOLEON I, slain by the sword at Waterloo and revived by NAPOLEON III, represents the Roman Empire or Daniel's Fourth Kingdom under its seventh revived headship, and that, along with the False Prophet or Papacy it goes into destruction at the Lord's advent.[24]

Once again, however, the linkages between biblical prophecy and contemporary political upheavals in France were to prove unsustainable.

English anti-Catholicism had, from the beginning of the century, inspired a range of missionary endeavours in Ireland,[25] and the mid 1840s saw a wave of militant proselytising activity in the west of the country. A major player in this crusade was the Rev. Alexander Dallas. Well-known in evangelical circles through his interest in eschatological ideas and his sermons on prophecy, Dallas was already familiar with the Irish scene when, in 1845, a gift of £3,000 enabled him to begin what he saw as his 'great work', inspired by the belief that

> one of the signs of the imminent return of Christ was to be great distress among the nations, and [that] the blessed of the Lord were to be those found engaging in the mission work to which the Bible called them.[26]

Supported by powerful figures such as the Duke and Duchess of Manchester at Tandragee and the Earl of Roden in County Down, as well as prominent English evangelicals, Dallas' work in Connemara led to the establishment of the Irish Church Missions in March 1849. Within four years he claimed to have over 300 agents working with around 5,000 children in his society. This aggressive crusade was, however, not surprisingly, beset by controversy and accusations of 'souperism'; causing considerable difficulties for local Protestant church leaders, it was in decline by the early 1860s.

By this stage, however, religious controversy of a different kind was becoming a common feature of life in the fast-growing northern capital of Belfast. The decline of the rural domestic economy and the parallel rise of Belfast as an industrial centre had brought an influx of migrants from the countryside, which not only changed the religious balance of the town's population in numerical terms, but also determined the nature of the relationship between the urban Catholic and

Protestant communities. The sectarian rhetoric and accompanying violence which had characterised relations between the two religions in the border counties of south Ulster in the late eighteenth and early nineteenth centuries was now frequently in evidence within the town. Community relations were not helped by the aggressive stance taken by evangelical open-air preachers who interpreted their religious duty in terms of direct confrontation with the 'Man of Sin'. A 12th of July sermon by Rev. Thomas Drew in 1857 typified the type of anti-Catholic rhetoric which all too often resulted in street rioting:

> Of old times lords of high degree, with their own hands, strained on the rack the limbs of the delicate Protestant women, prelates dabbled in the gore of their helpless victims. The cells of the Pope's prisons were paved with human gore and human hair ... The Word of God makes all plain; puts to eternal shame the practices of persecutors, and stigmatises with enduring reprobation the arrogant pretences of Popes and the outrageous dogmata of their blood-stained religion.[27]

The cancellation of such controversial street preaching was itself seen as dangerous defeatism in the ongoing war against an ever-threatening Catholicism. The *Belfast News-Letter* was in no doubt that the religious identity of its readers was in danger of being swept away:

> The Romish mobs have triumphed in our town. The preaching of the Gospel in our streets to the destitute, ragged poor, is put down. Belfast now ranks with Kilkenny, or Cork, or Limerick. In these Romish cities, where priests are regnant and their mobs omnipotent and the authorities bow to their behest, no Protestant minister dare lift his voice in the streets or highways to proclaim the peaceful message of the Cross – he would be stoned or murdered.[28]

While such polemics were confined to a vociferous minority of religious leaders, in every generation their vivid and graphic portrayals of martyrdom and violence have helped to sustain deep-rooted fears of the planned annihilation of Protestantism in Ireland.

On the other hand, the excitement generated by religious revivals within Protestantism also provided the opportunity to focus attention on the urgent need of spiritual preparation for the everlasting life, with the more pious and 'committed' sects particularly benefiting. The 'Great Awakening' of 1859, for example, saw significant increases amongst Baptists and an enthusiasm for Brethrenism which was 'to make Ulster one of the strongest centres of Brethren work'.[29]

The discourse of Dwight L. Moody, whose evangelistic tours in Britain attracted many thousands of eager listeners in the early 1870s was typical:

> I believe He is yonder, getting his guest-chamber ready, and the moment it is ready, those clouds shall roll away and He shall come, and we shall be caught up together to meet the Lord in the air.[30]

A trawl of religious material published in the second half of the nineteenth and first half of the twentieth centuries brought to light only scattered references to prophetic discourse in publications such as *The Church Advocate*, and a few individual examples of apocalyptic enthusiasm. The Rev. W.J. Christie, Church of Ireland incumbent of Lower Badoney from 1872 to 1886, and of Ardstraw from 1886 until 1905, for example, seems to have been particularly committed to disseminating the news of the imminent Second Coming amongst his parishioners.[31] Christie was honorary secretary of the Blessed Hope Union, 'an association of those who desire to be found unitedly waiting and watching for the return of the Lord Jesus', under whose auspices he published a wide range of publications. *Gospel Echoes*, for example, was a religious monthly 'devoted to Righteousness, Temperance and Judgment to come', which he edited and published himself. The name was changed to *Joy Bells* in 1885; designed to attract young readers, the new version was, however, no more successful than the original in covering the cost of production. Christie's constant references to an accumulation of 'signs in the heavens above and in the earth beneath' were more fully developed in pamphlets such as *Behold the Bridegroom Cometh* (Gortin, n.d.); *Notes on the Great Pyramid* (Gortin, 1881); *The Sanctuary Foresaken: a Sign of the End* (Gortin, n.d.) and *The Time of the End* (Gortin, n.d.).[32] In the latter publication Christie quotes from a range of contemporaries to substantiate his claims that the last days are at hand, interpreting numerous international occurrences, both human and natural, as the signs of prophecy, and calculating that the world would end in 1882. Needless to say, it did not.

Locally, late nineteenth-century political developments suggested that a major transformation was taking place within Irish society. Welcomed by nationalists, viewed with horror by a majority of Protestants, the possibility of Home Rule dominated both political

1886 Riots
Courtesy of *The Illustrated London News*

and religious discourse. On the one hand, Gaelic revivalists envisaged the dawning of a new age – a secular Utopia in which English modern and materialist influences would be swept away by a self-governing people embracing a vibrant, newly-awakened Irish culture. Protestant evangelicals were equally aware of the enormity of the consequences of the proposed constitutional changes in terms of their religious and cultural identity; in it they saw the destruction of all they believed most sacred. As the Methodist journal, the *Christian Advocate*, stated in 1886:

> Home Rule for Ireland means not only war against the Crown rights of England, but war against the Crown rights of Christ... its inspiration is religious antipathy, its methods plunder, its object Protestant annihilation.[33]

The language was by now familiar, but the danger to 'the faithful few among the faithless many – the loyal Sons of Judah amid the faithless men of Israel' seemed closer than ever.[34]

As we have seen, elements of millennial thought and activity can be identified at different stages of nineteenth-century Irish life, most particularly during periods of crisis. However, although theological debate could be both intense and divisive, amongst Catholics, and indeed at the popular level within Protestantism, the language and imagery of millenarianism could be utilised without any intellectual commitment to the concept itself. Increasingly as time went on, prophetic proclamations were more likely to be made by individuals who, while gathering around them an enthusiastic following, did not seriously impact on wider society. Although the new and serious challenge to the ascendancy of Ulster Protestantism gave rise to apocalyptic language, it was envisaged by political leaders of all colours that the battle to be fought would be by armed Volunteers. The strategic plans being made on both sides did not include intervention by heavenly hosts.

NOTES

1 PATRICK O'FARRELL, 'Millennialism, Messianism and Utopianism in Irish History', *Anglo-Irish Studies,* ii (1976), pp. 45–46, p. 53.
2 J.S. DONNELLY, Pastorini and Captain Rock: Millenarianism and Sectarianism in the Rockite Movement of 1821–4' in J. CLARK and J.S. DONNELLY (eds), *Irish Peasants and Political Unrest 1780–1914* (Manchester, Manchester University Press, 1983), p. 105.
3 SEAN CONNOLLY, *Religion and Society in Nineteenth-Century Ireland* (Dundalk, Dundalgan Press, 1985), p. 28.
4 KRAUSE to his sister, 29/11/1831, quoted in C.S. STANFORD, *Memoir of the Late Reverend W.H. Krause* (Dublin, 1854), p. 163.
5 D.N. HEMPTON, 'Evangelicalism and eschatology', *Journal of Ecclesiastical History,* 31, 2, (April, 1980), pp. 179–94.
6 KENNETH HYLSON-SMITH, *Evangelicals in the Church of England 1734–1984* (Edinburgh, T. & T. Clark, 1989), pp. 94–6.
7 ROY COAD, *A History of the Brethren Movement* (Exeter, Paternoster Press, 1976), p. 129
8 *Christian Examiner*, August, 1828.
9 *Christian Examiner*, August, 1828.
10 *Christian Examiner*, June, 1829.
11 *Christian Examiner*, May, 1828, September, 1835.
12 *Christian Examiner*, November, 1832.
13 *Christian Examiner*, May, 1834.
14 DESMOND BOWEN, *The Protestant Crusade in Ireland,* 1800–70 (Dublin, Gill and Macmillan, 1978), p. 65.
15 M. LANKTREE, *Biographical Narrative* (Belfast, 1836), p. 381. See also *Primitive Wesleyan Magazine* (March, 1834).
16 D.H. AKENSON, *Small Differences: Irish Catholics and Irish Protestants, 1815–1922: an International Perspective* (Kingston, McGill-Queen's University Press, 1988), p. 145.
17 CHRISTINE KINEALY, 'Potatoes, Providence and Philanthropy' in CHRIS MORASH and RICHARD HAYES (eds), *Fearful Realities: New Perspectives on the Famine* (Dublin, Irish Academic Press, 1996), pp. 140–171, p. 142.
18 Quoted in ROBERT DUNLOP, 'The Famine Crisis: Theological Interpretations and Implications', in MORASH and HAYES (eds), *Fearful Realities,* pp. 151–63, p. 166.
19 CARMEL QUINLAN, '"A punishment from God": The Famine in the Centenary Folklore Questionnaire', *Irish Review,* No. 19 (Spring/Summer, 1996), pp. 68–86, p. 72.
20 Quoted in SEAN RYDER, 'Famine and the Nation', in MORASH and HAYES (eds), *Fearful Realities,* pp. 151–163, p. 157.
21 MICHAEL BARKUN, *Disaster and the Millennium* (London, Yale University Press, 1974), pp. 63–4.
22 DESMOND BOWEN, *History and the Shaping of Irish Protestantism* (New York, Peter Lang, 1995), p. 265.
23 HENRY SEDDALL, *Edward Nangle: the Apostle of Achill; a Memoir and a History* (London, Hatchards, 1884), p. 229.
24 Ibid., p. 252.
25 DAVID HEMPTON and MYRTLE HILL, *Evangelical Protestantism in Ulster Society 1740–1890* (London, Routledge, 1992), pp. 80–102.
26 BOWEN, *History,* pp. 208–24.

27 Quoted in HEMPTON and HILL, *Evangelical Protestantism*, p. 124.
28 Quoted in A. BOYD, *Holy War in Belfast*, 2nd ed. (Belfast, Anvil Books, 1970), p. 39
29 MYRTLE HILL, 'Assessing the Awakening: the 1859 Revival in Ulster', in INGMAR BROHED (ed.), *Church and People in Britain and Scandinavia* (Lund, Lund University Press, 1996), pp. 197–213.
30 DWIGHT L. MOODY, quoted by W.J. CHRISTIE, *The Time of the End* (Gortin, n.d.), p. 15.
31 J.B. LESLIE, *Clergy of Connor* (Belfast, Ulster Historical Foundation, revised edition, 1993), p. 261.
32 *Gospel Echoes*, *Joy Bells* and these pamphlets can be located in the Linen Hall Library, Belfast.
33 *Christian Advocate*, 8 January 1886.
34 T. ELLIS, 'God and the Nation. A Sermon preached to the Orangemen of the District of Portadown in St. Mark's Church, Portadown' (Armagh, 1885).

Atomic bomb, Nagasaki, 1945
Courtesy of the Imperial War Museum

4
FAITH AND FEAR IN THE 20TH CENTURY

This is the battle of the Ages which we are engaged in. This is no Sunday School picnic, this is a battle for truth against the lie, the battle of Heaven against hell, the battle of Christ against the Antichrist.[1]

THE TWENTIETH CENTURY witnessed the most powerful demonstrations of the use and abuse of power by humanity. The terrible consequences of natural disasters, such as floods, earthquakes and famine have often been exacerbated by political and military considerations. War on a world-wide scale, ethnic cleansing, torture, cruelty and neglect provide a sombre backdrop to this technologically sophisticated age. The ability to clone animal life, to modify plant life genetically, and to replace vital organs in the human body, would have been considered nothing short of miraculous only a couple of generations ago. The speed of change, and our ability to view events on the other side of the world as they happen, have given rise to a sense of anxiety about the moral and ethical considerations of science, and about the direction in which humanity is heading. While one would expect a corresponding rise in millenarian activity in such a climate, the reality is not quite so straightforward.

Norman Cohn has provided an interesting interpretation of the two great movements of the first half of the century – Communism and

Fascism – suggesting that they can both be seen as forms of millenarianism. Each concept relies heavily on the complete annihilation of the enemy, construed in terms of economic or social division. In each instance, a New World is envisaged, cleansed and purified, reserved for the 'Chosen People'.[2] In contrast to these 'optimistic' views of a peaceful new era, however, was the prospect of man-made global catastrophe. Both world wars, and in particular, the use of atomic weapons at Hiroshima and Nagasaki, brought total world destruction into the realm of the possible. One did not need to belong to a small religious sect to envisage the world ending in flames and terror and, as Damian Thompson points out, when the prospect of nuclear war faded, pollution, global warming and the hole in the ozone layer provided frightening substitutes.[3] Entirely secular apocalyptic views now co-exist with the belief in mankind's accelerated progress. At the same time, the late twentieth century saw the flourishing of a new wave of millenarianism, embracing a variety of beliefs, from those of fundamentalist Christians – particularly in America – to the occult beliefs of those characterised as 'New Age'.

Within this framework, Ireland's own 'troubles' have been intermittently viewed from an apocalyptic or millenarian perspective, encompassing the hope that a free people would inhabit the new world. In 1914, for example, in the midst of the hysteria of war, the *Irish Review* published an article quite untypical of its usual sedate tone. Entitled 'The Messiah – a Vision', the piece, by Ita O'Shea, proclaimed that:

> The redeemer of Ireland was already born, and would soon lead the nation out of darkness into light. Although born in Ireland, he had spent most of his life outside the island. He was still under 30 and combined in his person the authentic glorious heritage of the Gaelic past and the capability of transforming Ireland into a modern society. ... He is the incarnation of the Spirit of Ireland – the heir par excellence of her Past – destined to be the dominating figure of the spacious days of her not so remote future.[4]

Patrick Pearse was soon to be identified as Ireland's saviour, and his messianic vision invested the Easter Rising of 1916 with Christian images of martyrdom and resurrection.[5] In the second half of the twentieth century, however, millenialism took a reactionary, rather than a revolutionary form, amongst Protestants in the north-east of

Ireland. As surveys have persistently shown, Northern Ireland has resisted the trend of secularisation so evident in other parts of the British Isles:

> For every denomination, members in Northern Ireland are much more likely than their co-religionists in Britain to have been born again, to be evangelical in theology, and to take a literalist view of the scriptures.[6]

Moreover, one of the major developments in terms of personal faith is the number of new religious denominations that have emerged over the past few decades. The last religious census in Northern Ireland detailed 71 groupings with ten or more adherents, including seven from non-Christian religions, suggesting that even within an overall trend of gradual secularisation, many still seek spiritual answers to the dilemmas of modern society.[7] The charismatic movement, for example, with its emphasis on the presence of the Holy Spirit, has proved popular in both Catholic and Protestant traditions, providing many with a 'personal, experiential and emotionally satisfying expression of faith'. The growth of some sects with a strong millennial tradition reflects both inward migration and the impact of international evangelising programmes. For example, both Jehovah's Witnesses and the Church of the Latter Day Saints (Mormons), originating in nineteenth-century America, have maintained a significant presence in Northern Ireland, with the former expanding from 83 in 1937 to 2,121 at the last census, while Mormons have grown from 71 to 1,437 over the same period; this despite the well-publicised anti-climaxes of predicted end-of-times by the prophets of both sects. The Baha'i World faith first made its appearance in the Northern Ireland census in 1961, with 32 adherents; by 1991 319 members were recorded, with ten Spiritual Assemblies and eight Local Groups scattered across the province.[8] Viny Robinson of the Baha'i Council for Northern Ireland explained the central thrust of this faith in a letter to the *Belfast Telegraph* on 22 February 1999:

> Baha'is believe that the breakdown in society is all tied in with the end of the Old World order and the New World order is now being spread in its place. The 'end of the world' is not the physical destruction of the earth but the end of the violence, inequality, prejudices etc. In other words, the establishment of the Kingdom of God on

> Earth that Christians are praying for.[9]

These are, however, tiny minority groups, representing only a small percentage of religious faith in a country in which the strength of Protestant evangelicalism remains particularly significant. Alwyn Thomson describes evangelicalism as 'an extended family', embracing a range of views from theologically conservative to radical.[10] At one extreme is a right-wing conservative tradition, which, while perhaps not numerically predominant, has a disproportionate influence on social and political as well as religious life in the wider community. While all Protestant denominations are agreed on the central importance of the Bible, the more extreme conservative positions reject modern interpretations, insisting on the literal truth of the scriptures. For them, the Bible is seen as 'being penetrable by the same routine methods of reading that we use for any other book', and thus the 'world of Bible writers and our world' are mutually comprehensible.[11]

Powerful preachers, proclaiming the daily relevance of the scriptures at tent crusades and in packed gospel halls as well as in more traditional church buildings attract large numbers for whom both the Old and New Testament prophecies hold the key to life itself.

The Whitewell Metropolitan Tabernacle on Belfast's Shore Road is a striking example of the contemporary strength of conservative evangelical theology. Completed in 1994 and seating over 4,000 in its major hall, this is the biggest church building in the country, attracting believers and witnessing conversions of men and women from a wide spectrum of religious or non-religious backgrounds. The Shore Road Tabernacle originated in an Orange Hall on the Whitewell Road in 1957, and there are now nine other churches at home and abroad, an impressive expansion, which is largely the result of the work of the dynamic Pastor James McConnell. The church's proclaimed purpose is

> none other than to preach the glorious gospel of the Lord Jesus Christ and the edification and preparation of God's people for the greatest event in history – namely the visible, physical, literal second coming of the Lord Jesus Christ, back to this earth and the ushering in of his Kingdom.[12]

One measure of success was a twelve-week series on the Second Coming during the closing weeks of 1998, which regularly packed the large new hall. Pastor McConnell's explanation was that people

> are feeling insecure, unhappy, they wonder what is happening to the world, who they can turn to. They want someone to put the light on again for us and I tell them that Christ is coming. He will put the light on once more.[13]

The view that the world is in crisis which will be resolved only by divine intervention is echoed by preachers of many denominations, but most particularly and specifically by those on the conservative wing.

The most notable of Northern Ireland's conservative evangelical denominations is undoubtedly the Free Presbyterian Church of Ulster headed by the Rev. Ian Paisley. A Baptist by background, Paisley became pastor of Belfast's Ravenhill Evangelical Mission Church, a bastion of fundamentalism, in 1946. Five years later, his intervention in a dispute between moderates and extremists (on the side of the latter) in Lissara Presbyterian church in Crossgar, County Down, led to the formation of the Free Presbyterian Church. With Paisley continuously at its head, the new denomination's initial membership of 92 had increased to over 12,000 by the 1990s. The spectacular growth of Free Presbyterianism, at a time when other Presbyterian groupings are either declining or remaining stable, owes much to the personal influence of Paisley – 'Man of wrath' – the epitome of militant Protestantism,[14] for whom the dramatic discourse of millennial ideology is particularly well-suited. A 1997 pamphlet exemplifies his oratorical style:

> It was God who made the clock of time and wound it up. It will be God's intervention that will cause the clock of time to cease its ticking for evermore. Time will not stop a minute too late or a minute too soon. It will stop on the split second of God's predetermination or predestination.[15]

What distinguishes Paisley from other religious leaders is that he is also the founder and leader of the Democratic Unionist Party, and his 'theologically conservative Protestantism is [thus] actively coupled to right-wing politics'.[16] In a country where secular politics have been dominated by religious division since its establishment, the linkage has important implications, for anti-Catholicism is central to Paisley's religious beliefs. This is a theological position – as Steve Bruce points out, 'anti-Catholicism is at the heart of Protestantism. It was Catholicism that the reformers were trying to reform!'[17] For many conservative evangelical Protestants in Northern Ireland today, for whom Catholicism remains the enemy in the world of secular politics, this theological reasoning carries particular resonance. Writing under the heading 'Who is our Enemy?' in the *Protestant Telegraph* in 1974, Paisley's analysis of the political conflict raised it to a battle of cosmic proportions:

> There are those who mistakenly analyse the Ulster situation in terms of social and economic factors, in terms of politics, or philosophies. These theories and analyses collapse because they ignore, deliberately or otherwise, the main key, and to us the most obvious factor: Protestantism versus Popery. The war in Ulster is a war of survival between the opposing forces of Truth and Error, and the principles of the Reformation are as relevant today in Ulster as they were in Europe in the sixteenth century.[18]

Following a tradition stretching back through the centuries, Paisley identifies the Papacy as the Antichrist, and interprets any threat to Ulster's Protestant and British heritage as part of a conspiracy predicted in the biblical prophecies. Thus the Treaty of Rome, which heralded the formation of the European Economic Union, was perceived as a religious and political confederacy predicted in Daniel 2: 1–45 and Revelation 17[19] – a papist superstate. Closer relations between Dublin and London, within this context, even led to Margaret Thatcher being dubbed an agent of the Antichrist. Following the signing of the Anglo-Irish Agreement by Irish taoiseach Charles Haughey and the British prime minister in November 1985, Paisley declared:

> We are seeing now the development of the final kingdom of the beast. It is going to gain momentum. ... in order to placate the South, in order to get the blessing of the European nations and America, we in this Province are to be the sacrificial lamb. There is far more in the Anglo-Irish Agreement, than we are even aware of, internationally. We have been sold on the altar of political expediency in the furtherance of the kingdom of the beast.[20]

The sense of engagement in a Holy War has intensified as the rate of political change within Northern Ireland has escalated in recent years. Just as he rejects the principle of ecumenicalism in religious life, so too Paisley rejects any notion of compromise in the political arena. In the cease-fires and political negotiations of the current 'peace process', Paisley sees only betrayal and treachery, and as Terence McCaughey points out, 'the sense of being trapped in a historical cul de sac encourages the notion that the end is at hand'.[21] With that end, will come reward for the faithful remnant:

> Are we mourning because sin is rampant in the wide world? Let us rejoice for our Lord has broken the dragon's head, and the day of vengeance must come when the Lord will overthrow the powers of darkness. Have we been looking with mournful spirit upon Old Rome and the Mahommedan imposture, and the power of Buddhism and Brahminism ... Let us be glad. Behold the Avenger cometh ...[22]

In a country where biblical language and symbols still have a steady currency, such rhetoric can also be used by those without a specific spiritual conviction to justify violent sectarianism. In October 1998, for example, *Ireland on Sunday* reported that a previously unheard of group calling itself the Red Hand Defenders admitted responsibility for, amongst other things, 'the cleansing of ten Roman temples and the burning of Catholic businesses in Portadown, Antrim and Newtownards'. The communication, which was signed 'Cromwell', made reference to Deuteronomy, 7: 2–7:

> ...Thou shalt smite them, and utterly destroy them; thou shalt make no covenant with them, nor shew mercy unto them ... ye shall destroy their altars, and break down their images, and cut down their groves, and burn their graven images with fire ... the Lord thy God hath chosen thee to be a special people unto himself....[23]

Alan Campbell, a graduate of London University and Head of Religious Studies at a high school near Belfast, is a prolific pamphlet writer on the millennial theme; he has lectured on Protestant and prophetic platforms throughout the United Kingdom, Canada, Australia and the USA. In his view, the various peace movements and initiatives of the early 1990s were 'sell-outs', and he urged his readers to 'Pray, not for Peace, but for Deliverance and Victory'.[24]

While such examples represent only a small strand of opinion, increasingly swimming against the tide, there is no doubt of the tension generated by a religious and/or political philosophy that draws on prophetic literature. With the Northern Ireland political scenario facing inevitable change, it is perhaps not surprising that the vulnerability of the increasingly marginalised should seek justification and comfort in the language of the faith that promises retribution and reward, and a prophetical doctrine which throughout history and across nations has provided a refuge for

> those suffering from a deep-rooted despair of the future, the marginalised, persecuted, oppressed and disillusioned – people who in the complete absence of political hope have turned to its pages for steel-clad justification that their sense of alienation is proof of their election.[25]

Both the reading of Ireland's past, and the plans for its future governance, seem to be inextricably bound up with other-worldly visions of destruction and renewal.

NOTES

1 IAN PAISLEY, 1988, Quoted in DENNIS COOKE, *Persecuting Zeal: A Portrait of Ian Paisley* (Dingle, Brandon, 1996), p. 4.
2 NORMAN COHN, *The Pursuit of the Millennium* (London, Temple Smith, 1993).
3 DAMIAN THOMPSON, *The End of Time* (London, Vintage, 1999 ed.), pp. 133–4.
4 *Irish Review*, January 1914, quoted in TOM GARVIN, *Nationalist Revolutionaries in Ireland 1858–1928* (Oxford, Clarendon, 1987), p. 76.
5 PATRICK O'FARRELL, 'Millennialism and Messianism in Irish History', *Anglo-Irish Studies*, ii (1976), pp. 45–68, p. 57.
6 STEVE BRUCE, *Religion in Modern Britain* (Oxford, Oxford University Press, 1995), p. 62
7 NORMAN RICHARDSON (ed.), *A Tapestry of Beliefs: Christian Traditions in Northern Ireland* (Belfast, Blackstaff Press, 1998), p. ix.
8 PAUL WELLER (ed.), *Religions in the UK: a Multi-Faith Dictionary* (Derby, University of Derby, 1993).
9 'Writeback', *Belfast Telegraph*, 22 February, 1999.
10 ALWYN THOMSON, 'Evangelicalism and Fundamentalism', in RICHARDSON, *A Tapestry of Beliefs*, pp. 240–62.

11 STEVE BRUCE, *Firm in the Faith* (Aldershot, Gower, 1984), p. 4.
12 *The Cradle, the Cross and the Crown: The History of The Whitewell Metropolitan Tabernacle*, 1994 .
13 Quoted in the *Belfast Telegraph*, February 1, 1999.
14 PATRICK MARRINAN, *Paisley: Man of Wrath* (Tralee, Anvil Books, 1973).
15 IAN R.K. PAISLEY, *The Rent Veils at Calvary* (Belfast, 1997), p. 61.
16 STEVE BRUCE, *Firm in the Faith*, p. 161.
17 Ibid.
18 *Protestant Telegraph*, Vol. 9, no. 2, 15 June 1974 (copies in the Newspaper Library, Central Library, Royal Avenue, Belfast).
19 STEVE BRUCE, *God Save Ulster: the Religion and Politics of Paisleyism* (Oxford, Clarendon, 1986), pp. 227-9.
20 *Revivalist*, December, 1986.
21 TERENCE McCAUGHEY, *Memory and Redemption: Church, Politics and Prophetic Theology in Ireland* (Dublin, Gill and Macmillan, 1993), p. 44.
22 *Revivalist*, February 1984.
23 *Ireland on Sunday*, October, 1998.
24 ALAN CAMPBELL, *For What Should Ulster Pray? A Biblical Response to the So-Called Peace Movements and Initiatives* (1993).
25 MARINA BENJAMIN, *Living at the end of the World* (London, Picador, 1998), p. 97.

A familiar Belfast image

Courtesy of the *Belfast Telegraph*

CONCLUSION

And it shall come to pass in the last days, saith God, I will pour out of my Spirit upon all flesh: and your sons and your daughters shall prophesy, and your young men shall see visions, and your old men shall dream dreams

Acts 2: 17

DESPITE THE DIFFICULTY OF RECONCILING 'natural' and man-made measurements of time, the approach of the twenty-first century stimulated public interest in all theories connected with the end of time. While most people would not identify with a full-blown millennial ideology, there is no doubt that the fast pace of late twentieth-century life, dominated by technological, medical and scientific breakthroughs, resulted in a wide-spread fear that the world is fast reeling out of its 'natural' orbit. Across Europe civil unrest and 'wars and rumours of wars' further promote a sense of instability, while within the six counties of Northern Ireland, the rapidity of change in the political landscape raises both hopes and fears.

In February of 1999, the *Belfast Telegraph* ran a short series on 'faith and fears in the run up to the millennium'. Tracing the traditions, quoting both extremists and the totally sceptical, the series was an early example of the obsessive interest in millennial ideologies triggered by the approach of the year 2000. While many ministers of religion took the opportunity to urge caution and common sense, the articles outlined the familiar position. Of more interest, perhaps, was the response of the general public in the 'Writeback' section of subsequent editions. Thus, on 5 February, J.R. Clarke of Newtownards restated the conservative evangelical position:

> ... the fundamental message of the Bible is that those who reject the Saviour will face the trials and tribulations to come.
>
> I appreciate that these simple views will be seen as bigoted or politically incorrect, or possibly damaging to the peace process, but people should be warned that the terrible events of the end will not end in death for those who, in Our Saviour's words, go away into everlasting punishment.[1]

Another 'Believer', however, put a modern spin on the prophecies, contending that the Old Testament was encrypted with a code recently deciphered by a computer. He claimed that 'encoded references to Shakespeare, Newton, Clinton, the Holocaust, the Gulf War, the man on the moon etc. all appear[ed] in the first 5 books of the Bible', and that 'leading mathematicians and top US National Security officials accept the Bible Code as fact'.

One could, of course, give many examples of millennial expression without proving that the ideology has had anything other than minimal influence in the late twentieth century. As already suggested, it appears as no more than an undercurrent, easily dismissed by rationale and logic, but powerful enough to inspire and sustain the vulnerable, and sufficiently adaptable to survive repeated miscalculations and the bad press of violent extremists. For, while the reasoning behind the ritual execution of 90 people at Waco in 1994 is beyond the grasp of most, there is no doubt that, as Derek Bingham declared in the *Belfast Telegraph*, 'the millennium opens up huge and searching questions ...'[2] Moreover, the resurgence of Pentecostalism and conservative evangelicalism across America and parts of Europe[3] indicates that fundamentalist Ulster Protestants are not alone in their belief that the final 'Signs of the End' are all around us.

NOTES

1 *Belfast Telegraph*, February 1999.
2 *Belfast Telegraph*, 4 February 1999.
3 DAMIAN THOMPSON, *The End of Time* (London, Vintage, 1999 ed.), pp. 139–66.